A Soul Cried Out for Meaning

K. L. Smith

Copyright©

Sophie - Melissa,

'Still, I dream of my future with you'

From 'Dream' (page 83)

'Suffering ceases to be suffering at the moment it finds meaning'

- Dr. Viktor E. Frankl

Contents

Ill Fated Energy

Ill Fated Energy	3
Let Thee Rhyme	5
It's Not My Fault	7
Prepare for War	9
I Will Cry	11
Shadows	13
New Scene	15
Seeing Death	17

Troublesome

Anger in Me	21
Red Apple	23
Two Wrongs	25
Exile	27
Catch Me if You Can	29
Remembering	31
Liberate Me	33
Keep Faith	35

Penetrating Words

Is There Really Now No You and Me	39
Penetrating Words	41
Tequila Rose	43
She Ponders	45
The Word Love	47
In Your Arms	49
I Hope Now Someone Loves You	51

Contents

Winds of Change

Eye in the Cloud	55
Waiting	57
Winds of Change	59
Feather of Paradise	61
Wild Winds	63
Free	65
Thy Will be Done	67
Shout of Creation	69

Into the Light

Into the Light	73
We Touch the Unseen	75
Two of a Kind	77
My Morning Muse	79
Music	81
Dream	83
Little Kicks Inside Her	85
Truth	87
The Aim	89
Live Forever	91

Dedication

Ill Fated Energy

Ill Fated Energy

In the aroma of a lilac scented garden

a manic majestic wonder explodes.

In an operatic chorus

I leap over sanities threshold.

Dancing with the spirits they permit to this

safety of euphoria.

Though an ill-fated energy,

conflicted with dysphoria.

Toxic venom of pain, coursing to the brain.

The demon's curse, glossed over by an

angel in verse.

Let Thee Rhyme

Indulge in the mystery, grasp the suspense.

Set sail in the search, hail the pretence.

Jump, hop, spring, like a harmonic choir let thee sing.

Where is the time that waits for no one?

Lying quiescent? If so, what from?

Plié, twist and dance,

in a tunnel of love let thee romance.

Will we meet in the after?

Once again bathe in past laughter?

Yours, theirs and mine.

A poetical lunatic let thee rhyme.

It's Not My Fault

It's who's fault I'm like this?

It's their fault it all goes to piss.

It's her fault it doesn't always sink in

it's his fault the thinkin' and thinkin'.

It's someone's fault my moods aren't here or there,

it's everyone's fault to finish what I start is rare.

It's Adams fault my temper is short,

it's your fault when I'm starboard to your port.

It's not my fault this passion, this rhyme,

it's not my fault but I'd take it every time.

Prepare for War

No rage to destroy, no pain on the heart to crush.

Futile my skills with pen and brush.

Does the spirit forsake?

The comfort to hear, riches to see,

still destitute I be.

No tears, no laughs, no screams and no prayers,

no energy in the trigger finger to let off the call flares.

Rain beats out a beating onto the white glass

as waves hit shore.

I would sooner cry a battle hymn

and prepare for war.

I Will Cry

I will cry until my tears overflow the rivers

and become lost to the seas.

I will cry until the deserts thirst is quenched

and raindrops drip life onto the barren.

I will cry until the angles pluck a melody

onto my poetic chords and they carry me home to rest.

Alone I cry, and like the frozen sea

I struggle to know the reasons why.

Shadows

The music stops and I feel the cold,

love carved and extracted.

Can the soul save itself

as they fight for my last breath?

Pulling me into the shadow world

where dead hearts can't bleed.

Moons don't reflect from seas,

and on the vulnerable, the shadows feed.

New Scene

When nimbus drift away,

the hissing of the sun

lights the path that leads the way.

Dimitri rises through the spine

reviving in a dream.

The realm of the soul the new scene.

From the depths, a cry

awakening to the truth

only when I die.

Seeing Death

Last one goes in, goes down

floor pressing hard against my unjustified crown.

Dazed, feeling out for the door

struggling, curled out on the floor.

Sweat, tears, body's being bled,

gagging, chocking, bloods being shed.

I shut my stinging eyes to deaths smile

as it attacks from inside I'm on capital trial.

Needing God's force to fight

evils pondering like a moth to a light.

They're laughing as I cry.

There's no one to hold me and kiss me goodbye.

Familiar voices in my head, somehow different instead.

Is it him? The one who satisfies in my sin.

Eyes lost in my cry, all alone I'm going to die.

The blood runs from my wrists to my palms,

then catching my eye, the new testament and psalms.

Troublesome

Anger in Me

In its hate I can love it

in my excitement it's a curse.

It searches me I crave it

I dig deep down in the purse.

Then it's there erupting in my pit,

this feeling so raw.

Red, no mercy, only blood is the cure.

I'm possessed, no control.

My mind now dark, black as coal.

Erratic what's coming, at will I could kill.

An emotion so frenzied

in need of much more than a pill.

Red Apple

Like the addict there's a craving,

appetite for the need.

Fantasies thriving, irritation for greed.

Summon a resistant so stunning too weak.

Redolence sweet, oh to taste the red apple treat.

Call on divinity. Interrogate the same faith.

Inside demand so unsafe.

Whirlwinds wisp a whisper of a needing inducing sin.

Ferocious, this conflict within.

Two Wrongs

I've heard two wrongs don't make a right.

I'm finding out the hard way tonight.

My soul in the fog could fade away.

He's got it coming I just can't let it lay.

Hung, drawn and quarter, like a ripper in the night

I have the urge, the need, the taste to slaughter.

If not his time but mine to go, I'm ready, let it flow.

A boy with a lion heart, retaliation is a yes!

One lonely mother will weep 'goodnight God bless'.

This life given we did not choose.

Round after round on every score card we lose.

Resenting the load, the taste now bitter.

Still I'll fight until the end, tonight I'm no quitter.

Emergency services don't yet know

what's going to happen.

Soon those blue lights will be flashin'.

Exile

It's just there, yet so far

will it listen once?

How many times can you

wish upon a star?

Will they exile me

to an unknown land?

With just the company of

a busker hand in hand.

In a search for meaning,

in a search for treasure.

Exile me from all of this pressure.

Catch Me if You Can

It's exciting being chased,

catching planes and living it fast

the thrill however just doesn't last.

Waiting every day without warning,

twitching at the door in the wee hours of the morning.

Pressure and strain pollutes the chemicals in my already

imbalanced brain.

Never thought I'd consider handing myself over,

only going out shooting like a soldier!

Deliberation dusk until dawn, for now I'm in charge,

I'm the overseer.

My conscience tells me I'm profoundly wrong

in the perfect shape of a tear.

I'm not the ginger bread man. Yes,

I ran, ran, ran, but please, catch me if you can.

Remembering

Feels like I've been here so long.

I strain to think back to when things weren't so wrong.

But all I see are my hands cuffed in a sweatbox.

So I strive even harder trying to forget about locks.

No! I'm in a cold court cell, and like a scared snail

I retreat alone into my shell.

Still thinking, endeavouring to remember.

All I can see is a man in a wig

dictating my future and how I'm going to live.

'Stand up! Sit down!'

Fixed on thinking is causing me to frown.

And then I remember, the girls, the beach, the sun,

back in the days when it was fun.

A freeing memory until this time has passed,

puts strength in my arms as I hoist the mast.

Liberate Me

The spirits dark not bright,

with locks and bars left to right.

There's sorrow in their cry's in the night they shout,

anguishing for the out.

I try and sleep as the doors are open in my dreams.

It's mourning in the morning,

realising it's not the truth that I've seen,

craving freedom like a fiend.

Shrouded in the smoke,

on its silver cloud I wish to float away.

Though here I'm succumbed.

Nothing free, not he, not me.

Stroke my heart and help me fight

as I lose the light from the dark of night.

Liberate me from this state of mind

liberate me from this place in time.

Keep Faith

I'm unsure why when I'm alone in this cell,

I start to dwell on heaven and hell.

Much I have lost within these four walls

lost, gone, insignificant to all.

Wanting right now as my mind is dense,

in this hole, this hole of belligerence.

Salvation from above can it really rescue me?

Before my soul drowns in this adversity.

The ringing of despair cannons of every wall.

Night after night of solitude

I get so confused, confused with it all.

However, my heart knows there's more,

so I turn to the cross and the mercy

of God I do pray for.

This perilous path however unsafe,

I'll drip away this stone I will always keep faith.

Penetrating Words

Is There Really Now No You and Me

The sun burst from the river flowing, not love that
caught my eye.
The days I cursed somehow inside did treasure,
our love that made me cry.
I need you here, why are you there?
How can you not care?
Enable this void while I walk a highway of troubled souls.
Bring the light of life.
I long for you like the blood of Christ.
The mist now leaves the river like the love from my
heart. You go on, you listen to the flesh.
Turn your back on love, turn your back on me.
Leave me here on my knees, to prey, beg and cry.
Girl please, look at me once more.
Watch my lonely heart through these eyes die.
I love you, I beg you, please don't let this be.
Who will you share your life with now, if not me?
There's my heart, now take my eyes as you in their arms
I cannot see. How did this slide?
Is there really now no you and me?

Penetrating Words

I fantasize of you wearing erotic lingerie

from the poetry you're portraying.

I probe the prose,

I know just what you're saying.

Cedillas on letters,

smooth curves of your words.

I want to bite the lid of this pen

making love to your poesy,

with my penetrating words.

Tequila Rose

She asked if anyone was sitting there.

Gladly and invitingly I said 'no'.

Her look was beautiful,

a bedazzling smile advancing

something inside of me.

There was dialog which I forgot

her elegance I did not.

She was tequila rose,

I the Lynchburg oak.

She said more with one look

than any word she spoke.

Warmth, emancipated by her soul,

melts away at the snow.

Revealing a taste

of what all want to know.

She Ponders

I seized onto those deep-seated eyes,

your deliberation, please from me don't hide.

I want all of you, let me dive into the tide fall

of the ocean inside.

The way she laughs excites me,

the way she ponders is seductive.

Like the tide, I'm drifting towards her,

and like the shore I hope she soaks me in.

The Word Love

You said the word love.

The way it was now never to return.

My heart parried, will my frailty let it all burn?

Can the two commit?

I scream my heart into the heavens,

the Lord knows I'm a hypocrite.

I would surely cry if we waved goodbye,

at least the thought of you and him would die.

Will the insecurities take off like a dove?

Then all my trust I can place in love.

In Your Arms

I'm in your arms

but I'm thinking of her.

Whatever this was has left my heart,

and I don't even care.

You kiss me tell me you need me,

but it's not your skin I crave.

We lie here naked,

but in her memory I bathe.

I Hope Now Someone Loves You

You once asked if I loved you

my short answer was 'no'.

The truth my feelings I could not let go.

I was dancing in the pink hue of the atmosphere,

escaping the dragon's fiery breath.

I could not see, I was deaf.

There have been now many moons

many of them blue,

I hope now someone loves you

and his love is true.

Winds of Change

Eye in the Cloud

She's a blessing, I've a gift the calling evades

to know is to love the eggs have been laid.

Eye in the cloud, must I be the ear?

I strain to listen; I try to write clear.

The eye in the cloud produces words from this pen,

my brain it sings, it does dance,

at times it forgets so give me a chance.

Let it gust in a hurricane, splash out the sea,

ignite the fuse, don't let it pass by me.

Bullets in the chamber a rattle in the heart,

I'll embrace with it, create with it.

There shall be no end, but a start.

Waiting

Like wintry trees waiting for their leaves to return,

I stand strong watching the tinder's burn.

Waiting in expectation with every folk-dance.

In waiting, do we diminish or do we enhance?

Tides wait for the moon once more,

do I labour on the wrong shore?

There's a weight in waiting to wait.

God please, I'm done with waiting.

Winds of Change

As caterpillar to butterfly I feel a change coming.

I surmise to bask in victory

as the Indian lotus springs to life.

Blowing in the wind, carrying excitement,

surfing on the sea change of optimism.

Like the woman at the well I feel its certainty.

I smell it in the petrichor dabbing myself dry.

After a thousand years I'm ready. Ignite the nest.

I am rising from these flames.

Feather of Paradise

Through the window and next to me graciously landing
a flawless white feather,
like on the morning of her funeral.
With the same strength compelling me to pause.
Calmly, needing no applause.
Reassurance those armies he built are falling.
Pirouettes in the breeze,
there all along even when I was crawling.
Alas, a resistance of a campaign of struggle,
spoken was the truth.
Verity, an end, brings a platitude of power,
like poems for a friend.
I was close to death but those closer.
A messenger of God, much more than a carer.
Remembering prayers of trust not tainted with why.
Nazareth be nigh! High into the mystic I soar.
Attend and hear, observe and behold,
digest the trumpets and wait for Gabriel.
Pronouncing durability into the unstable.
I drop arms stretched into the smoke that thunders.
Soaked in love, I resurface with the skulls of kings.
I have faith in the one He sent.
I accept what this feather of paradise brings.

Wild Winds

Wild winds blow hope throughout the west lands of Freedom.
In escaping the devils neck crank am I now the Dark Knight and not the Joker?
In a soprano high notes battle she touched me with divinity at the foot of Mount Zion,
that I am now brave enough to climb.
As a child of the creator I hunted those words of value.
So if she's the beauty,
I must undoubtedly be the beast she civilized.

Free

My reality I submit onto the spirit

as feelings form into tears.

With each tear I taste I realize again faith is sufficient.

It's difficult to accept matters of this world

flesh will more than condemn.

Hope slides seeming all to be lost.

His blood again will cleanse me; spirit lead me

where I need to stand.

Raindrops become my rhythm this world

can keep its merry band.

Through his painful attacks my arms

reached out in praise.

I need not a silver cloud nor even the wings of an angel

to remind me whom I serve, to know who is my Lord.

He was flogged and tortured.

He carried His cross, His blood shed for me.

I'm not imprisoned by guilt

but through His love like the truth,

I'm free.

Thy Will be Done

Every lip I kiss, every hand I hold,

I know to the earth will surely perish.

But with the light in those eyes life again I do cherish.

I wrench my rod free from these troubled waters

as her laugh blows again wind in my sail.

My line now gleams a knowledge of new skills

though they expect me to fail.

They trust in their chit chat; my trust is in faith.

Now is the time!

I know freedoms not free like those on the frontline.

It often embarks but I clip it away

though I cried I was proud of myself today.

My love, my acceptance, my care,

for her is unconditional, the best in all I've done.

I promise you my daughter, thy will be done.

Shout of Creation

Pen, paper, rocking chair

and a match.

It's time to create

inspiration to catch.

Like a river it's flowing

what's deep within bursts out.

Like a thief for his life,

from the gallows,

I shout.

Into the light

Into the Light

From obscure realms the whisper of

my conscience mutated into screaming.

Only gathering my cross carrying the load

when the soul cried out for meaning.

As the sun I arose the hero of the day,

victorious from the dark night's fight.

Beaming away insanity,

like a baby emerging into the light.

We Touch the Unseen

She's left much more behind

than a single blonde hair on my pillow.

Inspiration oozing, like rain overflowing

the leaves of a willow.

Feelings unchained as her absence is felt.

Flames of promises ignited from a kiss.

This night everything what's known

about her, I miss.

I realise every action now counts,

as this wave in me mounts and mounts.

I'm unsure what it is coming up

with the sun from over the horizon,

nor what to me you mean.

But I do know together,

we touch the unseen.

Two of a Kind

Lured in by the grace of a beaming smile,

that hid much.

I saw heartache through her eyes that I found attractive.

One kiss, two souls,

cut from the same cloth.

With those three words she made me whole.

A profound force struck something inside of us.

Beneath my fury and her pain,

like the thyme that grew through pebbles

we found love.

Some have their opinions, but I have her.

Others point their fingers

whilst mine flow through her hair.

Their noise though turns to music

as I hold her tight.

With each embracing note I motion to the light.

On the count of four our paths aligned.

The world hates,

we're two of a kind.

My Morning Muse

I awake in the calmness of tranquil poetry.

Protected in love, time losing all grip over me.

Music notes dancing in a gentle summer breeze

I'm like a loose leaf from a tree, not a care roaming free.

You are the poetry. With the bells that chime

my hand composes your fate to rhyme.

The way you motion with the mop,

you became my morning muse.

Alexa is taking requests in the kitchen,

so take my hand and I'll let you choose.

Music

To hear music is to feel.

Changing of emotion

echoing the expression of one's soul.

Proof of His existence.

Life without music, impossible.

Above clouds racing through veins

in musical notations love thrives.

Pulsating to the symphony of our lives.

Dream

You were once only a dream that I had.

I was a meandering river

gushing towards your valley of still,

turned the elixir of life.

As the dreamers dream, now you're to be my wife.

Dreams like you are beautiful.

But where do dreams begin?

Is it on the strings of harps and violin?

In the light of never failing love,

dreams believed come true.

Still, I dream of my future with you.

Little Kicks Inside Her

As we watch the birch logs burn,

little kicks inside her, excitement strikes!

Imagine I hadn't had been there,

no looks from the bandstand, smiles in the park.

Fire light and little kicks, emblems of hope in the dark.

Aspirations rise with the smoke,

the heir to my words until his eminence bespoke.

Truth

I listened to myself, I felt fake,

contributing fraud in a world corrupt.

In betraying myself, on my soul I invited disruption,

as deceit breeds with corruption.

In Lucifer's lies you live in hell

a cursed world of repression.

Your character has more to discover,

in the truth there's progression.

Bending reality becomes unbearable.

Have courage in electing your pathway,

in confusion let the truth portray.

I walked towards reality, my spirit strengthened,

from the depths I returned.

I tolerated the truth, and falsehood was spurned.

The Aim

In identifying the aim,

I bargained with the future.

I built an arc giving up the unworthy

and sailed away from a fool's paradise.

I paid a price, things improve with sacrifice.

Showing no weakness when preparing for war.

Acknowledging the violation of myself

when finally encouraged to explore.

I realised a steep climb up is meaningful.

In not listening to them,

I headed somewhere better, I went again.

Chaos turned into order, when I overcame the shame.

Vengeance or transformation?

The latter now the aim.

Live Forever

As I sailed the ocean of ignorance, I saw ahead of me

an uncharted land of treasure. But wild beasts roam.

Setting aside my fears I direct the helm towards,

despite yearning the comforts of home.

In changing my aim my anguish is eased

even though the beasts now prowl.

Although only opportunity I hear in their howl.

Menacing roars of turmoil ring.

Their grip loosening from the powerful truth.

I unsheathe my sword. I venture for meaning, and

to regain what was stolen in my youth.

In the assault the beasts devour,

but on my malevolence not my nobility.

Then there gleamed the treasure, as I cracked

open the chest of responsibility.

In victory I rested.

An oasis of calm concludes this endeavour.

I carve my words upon a stone.

My words will live forever.

Charlotte - Leigh
1991 – 2011

SmithShinepoetry.UK.

Printed in Great Britain
by Amazon